■SCHOLASTIC

News
Nonfiction Readers®

Our Earth
Helping Out

by Peggy Hock

Children's Press®
An Imprint of Scholastic Inc.
New York Toronto London Auckland Sydney
Mexico City New Delhi Hong Kong
Danbury, Connecticut

These content vocabulary word builders are for grades 1–2.

Content Adviser: Zoe Chafe, Research Associate, Worldwatch Institute, Washington, DC

Reading Consultant: Cecilia Minden-Cupp, PhD, Early Literacy Consultant and Author, Chapel Hill, North Carolina

Book Design: Simonsays Design!
Book Production: The Design Lab

Library of Congress Cataloging-in-Publication Data
Hock, Peggy, 1948–
Helping out / By Peggy Hock.
   p. cm.—(Scholastic news nonfiction readers)
Includes bibliographical references and index.
ISBN-13: 978-0-531-13831-1 (lib. bdg.) 978-0-531-20431-3 (pbk.)
ISBN-10: 0-531-13831-3 (lib. bdg.) 0-531-20431-6 (pbk.)
1. Energy conservation—Juvenile literature. I. Title. II. Series.
TJ163.35.H62 2008
363.73'5—dc22   2007051900

7 8 9 10 R 18 17 16 15 14 13 12

CONTENTS

Word Hunt 4–5

Caring for Earth 6–7

Keeping Air Clean 8–11

Saving Water 12–13

Making Less Trash 14–15

Getting Together 16–19

Save Earth While You Shop 20–21

Your New Words 22

What Can You Do Here? 23

Index 24

Find Out More 24

Meet the Author 24

WORD HUNT

Look for these words as you read. They will be in **bold**.

air pollution
(ayr puh-**loo**-shuhn)

gasoline
(gas-uh-**leen**)

litter
(**lih**-tur)

carpool
(**kar**-pool)

faucet
(**faw**-sit)

recycle
(ree-**sye**-kuhl)

shade
(shayd)

Caring for Earth

Do you ever help take care of things at home or in your school?

Did you know you can also help take care of your whole planet?

You can help take care of Earth's air, water, and land.

Did you ever help out in a garden? To grow food, you need clean air, water, and land.

You can help keep the air clean by taking fewer car trips. Cars cause **air pollution** when they burn **gasoline**.

Taking fewer car trips can cut down on pollution. Riding your bike or joining a **carpool** can help.

air pollution

gasoline

These kids came to the game in a carpool! If they came in separate cars, it would make more pollution.

Trees help clean the air of some kinds of pollution. That makes the air fresher and better to breathe.

Trees also keep you cool by giving you **shade**.

shade

Talk to adults about planting trees near your home or school.

Using less water is another way to help out Earth.

Check your water **faucet** to see if it leaks.

How else could you save water in your home and outside?

faucet

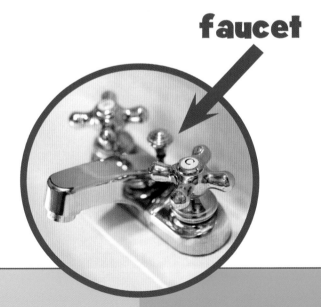

Save water by turning off the faucet while you brush your teeth.

Did you know you can also help Earth when you shop?

Try to buy only the things that you really need.

Why? Because someday, many of the things you buy will become trash.

Earth already has too much trash.

What will happen when there is no room for more trash here? People will need a new place to dump trash.

You don't need to work alone to help out Earth.

Clean up **litter** with friends.

Remind classmates to reuse and **recycle** paper, plastic, and metal.

Together, you will find lots of ways to help out.

recycle

Some groups get together to clean up litter. You can talk to adults about how to do this safely.

Talk to adults about ways to help out.

Can you use less energy at home and at school? That would help cut down on air pollution.

Maybe you could take a field trip to learn more about where your trash goes.

Do you have other ideas for helping out?

You can learn more about where trash goes by visiting a recycling center.

Save Earth While You Shop

1

Talk to an adult about buying cleaning products made from natural and safe materials.

2

Look for packages that can be recycled when you are done with them.

5

Get shopping bags that you can use again and again.

4

Talk to an adult about using energy-saving lightbulbs like this one.

3

MADE FROM ★ PLASTIC BOTTLES ★ RECYCLED

Look for products made from recycled materials.

YOUR NEW WORDS

air pollution (ayr puh-**loo**-shuhn) harmful materials that make the air dirty and unhealthy to breathe

carpool (**kar**-pool) a group of people who travel together to school, work, or other places

faucet (**faw**-sit) an attachment to a pipe that lets water out

gasoline (gas-uh-**leen**) liquid fuel that is made from oil found underground

litter (**lih**-tur) papers, cans, or other garbage thrown on the ground

recycle (ree-**sye**-kuhl) to make old plastic, paper, glass, and metal into new objects

shade (shayd) an area that is in shadow because a large object blocks the sunlight

WHAT CAN YOU DO HERE?

Think of ways you could help Earth in these places.

Home

School

Local park

Yard

INDEX

air, 6
air pollution, 4, 8, 10, 18

biking, 8

carpooling, 5, 8
cleaning products, 20

faucets, 5, 12
field trips, 18
friends, 16

gasoline, 4, 8

land, 6
leaks, 12
lightbulbs, 21
litter, 4, 16

metal, 16

packaging, 20
paper, 16
plastic, 16

recycling, 5, 16, 20, 21
reusing, 16, 21

shade, 5, 10
shopping, 14, 20–21
shopping bags, 21

trash, 14, 18
trees, 10

water, 6, 12

FIND OUT MORE

Book:
Guillain, Charlotte. *Cleaning Up Litter*. Chicago: Heinemann Library, 2008.

Website:
Act Green—Scholastic.com
http://www.scholastic.com/actgreen/

MEET THE AUTHOR

Peggy Hock lives near San Francisco, California. She likes to go backpacking in the mountains of the Sierra Nevada with her husband and two grown children. They always carry reuseable water bottles.